# SECOND LINE

a sequence

# SECOND LINE

a sequence

## Al Maginnes

REDHAWK
PUBLICATIONS

Second Line: A Sequence

ISBN: 979-8-89933-005-6  (Paperback)

Library of Congress Control Number: 2025945906

Cover Design (Art): Robert T Canipe
Book Design: Robert T Canipe

Printed in the United States of America.

First printing 2025.

Redhawk Publications
The Catawba Valley Community College Press
2550 Hwy 70 SE
Hickory NC 28602
https://redhawkpublications.com

## Note

This sequence began as elegy for my friend Allison Thompson who died at the first of February 2024. Allison was a writer, an actress and singer, a DJ, part of a special group of students, musicians, artists and would-be artists, bartenders, visionaries, time-wasters and misfits who populated Greenville, North Carolina and populated my universe in the late 1970's and early 1980's. Many of my closest friendships date from those years. These sonnets were all pretty much written during the last week of February 2024.

The cover art is a pastel drawing by David Early Larson, another friend from those years and a dear friend of Allison's. The name of this drawing is titled "Sadlack's." Sadlack's was a legendary watering spot in Raleigh, now sadly gone. Thanks to Philip Larson, David's brother, and Susan Crane, the artwork's owner, for permission to reprint. Those interested in David's work should visit the website Raleigh Rambles.

Sonnet 7 appeared in Avalon Literary Review.

This book, like all my work, is dedicated to my wife Jamie and my daughter, Isabel. This collection is also dedicated to friends and family who have sustained me over the years. Undying love and gratitude to each of you.

1.


If you should die in New Orleans, you can

rest knowing you will not go quiet. Friends,

musicians, hired mourners, people with

nothing better to do than follow the hearse,

will sing all the way to your grave and say

what a good soul you were, granting you

a measure of sainthood in this world

now that you have moved on to the next.

Everyone will sing "Saints" and "St. James

Infirmary," maybe even "Dying

Crapshooter's Blues." But if your time approaches,

it's good to have a request for the band to play.

I have a playlist so long, no one will stay,

my ashes will resurrect before it's done.

Second Line

2.


Maybe this is why funerals remind me

of jazz, not the tin pan alley shout of ragtime

or  Disneyland march, but slow embers of

a saxophone burning a melody's edge,

light pulsing at the hem of a galaxy,

how the musician's breath exalts and is

exalted by passage through the burnished

tubing, tempered until it turns the simple

exhale into something holy or almost holy.

One rainy afternoon, I sat in a now-dead friend's

house and tried to learn something about jazz

from her records, one after another

without knowing who I was hearing, a day

forgotten until now. I don't know why I was there.

3.


That friend died, as I said above. There was

no second line for her who loved music and dancing.

Those of us left to call each other with

every departure, work now to keep

the dead from our tongues when we talk, but our pasts

are longer than our futures at this point, so

the dead arrive, remembered and unbidden.

This is growing older in America.

We're clutching at every straw and every sweet note,

our bodies trying to bargain with time

while flesh plays soul and desire against

the middle where we can't stay too long because

at some point the old parts just say enough

and stop to fall. The flesh labors to rest.

Second Line

4.

It's common conversation in our house:

someone mentions a musician or actor's death

and usually one of us says "I thought they were

already dead." These days word flies so fast

I've been alerted to Sam Shepard's death

four times since he actually died. Sometimes I wish

someone had cast him as Chet Baker,

one American monument to excess,

whose trumpet could purr like the loneliest

animal alive on a planet that hosts

too much loneliness, where too many horns lie

locked in pawnshops. Sam Shepard and Chet Baker

and that movie was never made

and, as far as I know, never dreamed of.

5.

Maybe you were just home from work, opening

a beer when you got the news. Maybe a phone

wakes you in the middle of the night. And when

the world tips and cracks ever so slightly,

when again you must wait for balance,

maybe you understand one more time

that life is essentially improvisation,

routes to navigate without charts or maps,

things we wade through like weeds that grow

lush and high throughout the south, places

where no hidden grave seems likely. Sometimes,

if I pause in my walking, I swear

I can hear a band practicing through the trees,

but I can never tell what songs they're playing.

Second Line

6.


When she put on the flapper hat, she could

have been F. Scott's Jordan. Later she was Joplin

in a picture from a party I didn't attend.

Photographs took effort then. Phones were for houses,

not pockets. Whole years went undocumented.

Now we rely on memory, that faltering

witness, to explain our lives to us, though

we know how unreliable she is, prone

to twisting the narrative, of letting

the mourners walk before the hearse, the way

a second line commands more attention

than the deceased, playing the whole way to the grave

to interrupt the preaching and say the life

we ran from is exactly the one we lived.

7.


We were raised walking in line, learned early

to find our place and stay there so we could

be easily found for the rest of our lives.

We colored inside the lines, queued up for

concerts, for weddings where the bride refused

to be kissed, even though one New Year's Eve,

she and I shared a kiss that sprawled  from one year

to the next. Behind us, a band started

and we stopped kissing so we could sing. The tune

grew louder at the parts we didn't know,

where the real music lives, the parts of us

that want order and draw lines to keep

everyone going in the right direction,

forgetting old parties so we might keep order.

8.

There's a school of thought that says we choose

the life we are born into, that some gift

of prophecy skin is not capable of

decides this body at this particular time.

I know of Buddhist lamas who said

where and as who they would reincarnate.,

and it seems an attractive idea until

news is another day of bombs in Gaza,

battles in Ukraine, a classroom raked

by gunfire somewhere in these borders.

Who would choose that fate, given a choice,

but how many rise and dress each day,

leave to go about their business,

expecting that this will be their day for sudden death?

9.

Blues for Pluto who lost planetary status

about the time I turned fifty and became

obsolete in the eyes of those who would

make the world so efficient anything

and finally anyone can be replaced

by devices whose workings are so obscure

only the ones who repair them still work with tools,

not apps or downloads. Perhaps as we age,

our orbits grow more elliptical, offsetting

the plans that prescribe a certain way of motion.

From my own pocket of shadows, I'm rooting

for you, Pluto, as the debate cycles back

and forth over your status, and wise men

line up to look again in the telescope.

Second Line

10.


Maybe it was some flunky of the underworld

who beckoned us, two fifteen year olds in the coats

and ties our parochial school required

even as they gave us two hours to walk

through the French Quarter. In those days, I made

a story with each step (I still do).

Better one of hell's castoffs than a drunk

earning his daily drams luring sidewalk traffic

into the dark doorway he sprouted from.

Inside, glasses, leaning men, a dancer

no one was looking at. The invitation

came too early. I'd cross a span of years

before I found my spot to stare inside

and drink the dancers around me invisible.

11.


New Orleans is a gesture on my part,

a swamped in pocket of romantic ruin,

a place disinherited princes and poets

might drink their way through the great kingdoms

of story that makes the foundation

of all places humans gather. Death,

sadly, is no gesture, only the final

subtraction of an existence already set

on whittling us down beyond function

to bone and less than bone. I have no advice

about where to find the town's best coffee

or a restaurant that won't leave you broke

and swollen with heartburn. My New Orleans

is conjured. I invent every place I go.

12.


If I played guitar as well as I'd like to,

I'd never write another word, never have

anything to do with language, that sneaking

bastard stepchild, its betrayals and words

that won't quite say what they mean. Returning

to the old texts, we see how this sentence

speaks now as opposed to its day of writing

now that the landscape has changed. Each landscape

has its dead. You look seven or eight decades,

a few lifetimes, across corn or tobacco fields

and see a few graves in the crops' middle.

Winter makes them monuments, stark apparitions

in brown and gray weather bearing a scrap

of verse to live for all time with the deceased.

13.

The ones gone from this world return at

strange times for their visits, showing up

in the aisle of the grocery store, picking

between cans of soup, driving in the lane

next to us, standing in the backyard when

we wonder why the dog is barking. They don't

stay long, vanish with our first motion

or breath. Even if we remain still as bone,

they vanish. I'm not sure they have much

to share with us anyway. A few descriptions

of landscapes we don't have vocabulary

enough to believe in, one more reminder

that there are things that have nothing to do

with us, and the dead are one of those things.

Second Line

14.


When my imagination was larger,

WZZQ brought most of what I know

about the world into the bedroom

where I could dream lifetimes without moving.

One night Dr. John sang "Walk On Guilded Splinters,"

a swampy vamp that took a while to sink in.

First you fall in love, then you go the places

love tells you to go. How do you know

the first time you see her that she is the one

you will wake up next to more than half

your lives later? But maybe in the first

flicker, something is kindled, a call and response

like I heard from Dr. John and his singers,

voices that sounded like they called from a grave.

15.


I've said I hear music in the landscape

around here. Some afternoons wind carries thick

horn riffs from the college marching band.

Sometimes I hear organs or drums through trees

faceless as pedestrians. I can't be sure

if I truly hear this or if it's just hope

for something more than music promises.

It might be one way of softening the whine

and percussion of this city where I came

planning to stay a year. Maybe two.

Now I'm fluent in the backroads and where

to get cheap gas. Now I know how a place

changes one piece at a time while I tell myself

I can still name the music in the trees.

Second Line

16.

Is place one more abstraction? Like spirit?

Like soul? Like the dream someone insists

on explaining to you. But more have suffered

over the notion of place, however

misbegotten, than anything else except perhaps

money or love, companion abstractions.

We can talk long enough to reduce

everything to nothing but dust and less

than dust. But abstractions don't risk their lives

to cross a fence crowned with barbed wire

that marks a border people die to reach

or to guard. Drones deliver missiles

that blow men from their dreams into this world

where abstractions kill quicker than knives.

17.


Bobby Charles left Louisiana, but

Louisiana stayed on his tongue like good sauce.

If you think you haven't heard him, he wrote

"See You Later, Alligator" and "Walkin'

To New Orleans." And he made one great record

in Woodstock while he hid out from a pot bust

down home. It was a good place to record

because every player in town was waiting

for Dylan to unretire. Even lost

in the green hills of New York, there was still

gumbo and okra enough in his voice

to weld notes he couldn't play and chords

he couldn't name to melodies that should

have carried him further than they did.

Second Line

18.


I'm writing this from the weird spell when

winter—or what we call winter around here—

slides into the opening of spring.

We'd like to set the plants outside but know

how unpredictable nights can be, how

quickly cold can scorch life from a plant.

I'm thinking about planting a garden,

a real one this year, distraction from

from this new era that subtracts us

and the thought of flowers and vegetables

on the vine console like the real thing might.

But some tasks should be done without onlookers,

so I'll spare you my shovelwork, my unlikely sweat.

19.

I've heard of condemned men forced to dig

their own graves. And I have wondered, why

do the assassin's work? But I know

hope is always the last thing we surrender,

and those about to die labor because

the splinters in their hands, the morning cold

shredding as the sun asserts itself,

the curses on the edge of their hearing say

they are alive. And while they live, there might

arrive a message saving them all.

One man knows that Dostoevsky was saved

from a firing squad and went on to write

his great books. So he digs, dreaming about

the books he might write if only he survives.

Second Line

20.


It's easy, sometimes too easy, to get lost

when you're walking even when you follow

a funeral procession or a parade.

Something beckons your vision and you're off

on your own parade, walking through

one door, then another, until you never

return to the place you started. I say this

because I have wandered off from all

I had planned to talk about. Plans don't,

usually, go according to plan.

So I keep walking, looking for a spot

we recognize, some place we could find

a spot to stand and see our actions mapped out

arranged, as if we always knew where we were going.

21.

The greater your age, the longer the past.

The more that piles up around you or

gets left for the ones that come after you.

Forty years of notebooks saved in boxes,

filled with ink and never looked at again.

A thousand books I've read, more I will read

someday. However vast the plains behind us,

there is still a future to harvest.

That is what we count on, even while phones

fill with news of friends gone into hospice,

fallen to stroke or cancer, not the suicides

or car wrecks or overdoses that got us when

we were younger. The past is vanished

but there is still a place to put my feet.

Second Line

22.

When Louis Armstrong was hamboning on TV
and singing "Hello Dolly," I didn't know
about "West End Blues, which gives me chills
each time I hear it, that sets me down on streets
swirled by fog, Armstrong's horn a soft finger
pointing the way through the unchronicled winding
of streets with no signs to say their names,
so we can't say where we are, just as we can't
speak again to any of those friends with whom
we never said all there was to say, the way
Armstrong sings the melody when he knows his horn
won't say it any better, but he wants you
and all the friends you can no longer speak with
to walk Canal Street with him one more time.

23.

By now shouldn't we know more than we do?

We know the words to the songs and can clap

along in most cases, but when it's done

I'm never sure if it was what I was meant

to hear or if I spent the concert staring

at the fake velvet stage curtains, shifting

like breath as the stage lighs did their routine,

a choreography stage hands worked long

before electricity was anything but

a rumor lodged in the front lobes

of some necromancer willing to turn

from his dark craft to court the thing he believes

will allow control over fire, the one

element that is more than the dead can reach.

24.


All the new fiction conjures fresh worlds

rising from the ashes of this one.

My problem is surviving the battles,

the conflagrations and stupid errors

humans make and ignore until all

we relied on is falling apart. If

we get through that and I'm able to walk,

I'd be happy to ditch the scene here

for some promise of a finer existence.

The problem is that what got us here doesn't die

or learn from experience. So worlds will

always rise and fall, some faster than others,

and for some the tale of ruin is the landscape

they prefer, the falling, but not the rising.

25.


I've always felt myself one step behind

the world, and I suspect it will be

the same if there is any existence

beyond this one. And how sure can we be

we are experiencing this one properly?

So it will be in the next. And what comes

after that. It's hard to imagine any

state of being that doesn't allow change.

Sometimes, on the edge of orgasm, riding

the rush of some drug, even running

until the body vanishes into breath,

time can unravel. But the old machine

always catches up with us, pushes us

back in rhythm without our notice.

Second Line

26.


This weekend another memorial

I should attend. Death, it seems, is winning.

This is where I fall short. I fade away

when times get dark, recalling how little

I had to say after weeks of doctors

and hospitals, after coming home with

titanium in my spine, stainless steel

to hold it all in place. When death visits, it brings

too much company along. They crowd close

at services and celebrations to honor

the newly dead, stay behind for one more

at the bar after I leave. They'll be there

at the next gathering. And when they song start

the old songs, we will sing with them.

27.


Tell it to the trumpeter who doesn't

feel like practicing today. Tell it to

the man trying to limber his back enough

to work today. Tell it to the nurse

slow walking the last hour of a shift

that started fifteen hours ago.

Tell it to the one whose shaking hands raise

the day's first drink, the one that quiets the snakes,

to a mouth that speaks little beyond

the syllables commerce makes necessary.

No one remembers praying recently.

Not the birds fluttering to branch to ground

and back. Not the coffee drinkers who hear

the day's first hard strains of trumpet

Second Line

28.


Though we are born from it, we are afraid

of dirt. Before we can walk, we are told to wash

our hands before eating, our bodies before

or after sleep, in hopes our souls—

we believed in souls then—would stay clean

as well. And like dirt, we learned to stir

things around to hide what we don't need others

to know. If you can live without secrets,

you're better off. I'm not sure most of us

get that far. I once helped uncover

a skeleton buried a foot deep for

three hundred years. Every family has one

who has done time or been married

eight times, a past that sticks harder than dirt.

29.


I've planned my own vanishing often enough

that I've run out of plans. All my escapes

are the same anyway. I end up somewhere

I don't love, living a nameless life

too much like the life I live now. In these dreams,

I can drink again, a sign this fantasy

is bad for me. The longer it goes on,

the further I vanish through a series

of doorways and alleys, narrow lanes where

a body turns more to spirit each day.

For all I know, it might be a crime now

to walk out of one life and into another,

one you've never tried before, that shocks you

because it knows how to fit so well.

Second Line

30.


Johnny Thunders died in New Orleans.

Thirty five years later, no one knows how

or why. So now he is one more spirit

sliding through cemeteries, smoking cigarettes

in corners we can't get to. Watching drinkers

walk out of bars and improvise uncertain

paths to hotel or home. A last cold swallow

of coffee sits in a cup he would drink from

if he could. Like most ghosts, he doesn't speak.

Sometimes I think I should have bought the disks

I found in a punk record store right after he died,

but we always confuse what will stay constant

and what will not, like guitars and fame stained

with the ones too eager to believe you will die.

31.

While a scholar explains the history

and heritage of the second line,

I'm searching for my James Booker bootlegs

and trying to recall whether Professor Longhair

is stashed under P or L. It's not

that history doesn't speak to me, but the pact

music makes with the listener—this moment

matters—speaks louder. I've sunk more than one

small stanza by loading it with more information

than it could bear, and it went to the place

bad writing goes. Sometimes no music fits

the moment, but it plays anyway, doing its job

while I do mine. The dead deserve their songs.

It doesn't matter who sings them.

32.

We think we are well supplied until

we aren't. Sooner or later, we run low

on everything—money, dignity, time,

memory, which is simply one more kind of time.

Sometimes we don't have much to run out of,

one more indignity in a world

that sometimes seems to work overtime on

deprivation. Which makes anger. We remain

ready to attack even when no target

is clear, and it's hard to say why we're mad.

Fear justifies any action claim those skilled

at parsing human behavior. Or any

lack of action. The easy part is claiming fear.

Then comes the naming and the facing.

33.

There is no time of day set aside

for conversations with the past. Lately

these visits come more frequently than

I'm comfortable with. I want to drink

a cup of coffee, walk down Blount Street,

and I'm back to being lost in an airport.

I was nine. When I heard a voice telling me

where to meet my parents, I ran there.

The kid whose name was just on the intercom.

I'm driving my parents' station wagon

for the first time in gray Sunday rain,

and I miss the exit I need to take.

We only have to live any part of it once,

but once we've lived it, we are never done with it.

Second Line

34.


I'm turning the corner on this fixation.

Or so I think. Berryman thought he was

done with Dream Songs, but they fell from his pockets

for the rest of his life. Even walking to

his appointment on that bridge, he might have

been in dialogue with Henry or Mr. Bones.

You can't read the thoughts of the ones walking past,

though cell phones have allowed us all to hear

more than we ever needed to. One more

excuse for earbuds, but there are times

thoughts intrude so insistently music

is not a blessing but a distraction.

One distraction then another brings me

closer to learning what I'm trying to say.

35.


All the little preparations. The knife

stroked sharp. Strings of instruments twisted

into tune. Peppers and onions diced for

the skillet. Waking up and making sure

you know where you are. Someone laid out

the dark suit, polished the shoes like blades,

little gleams of light winking from burnished leather.

Pull the knot tight. We have reason

for dark cloth today. Each little task gains

gravity when you're getting ready for

something else. Today it seems important

that everything fit perfectly. Today,

tears, the ground opened, the words we murmur

and try to believe in the absence of music.

## Second Line

36.


Last time friends gathered for dinner, I paused

over which shirt I should wear, something

I seldom do, yet in so many old photos

we're wearing ties pulled askew, dresses made

for ballrooms and dance floors. Kids playing

dress up though we were technically grown.

One more way of not taking life seriously,

of letting the world continue all

the important business that goes on while

we're busy laughing. There were nights we danced

like we might be anyone other than ourselves.

We won't dance like that again. Time makes us

cautious pedestrians, waving good night

to old friends while we search for our car.

37.


Here we are, meeting ourselves on the cold drive

back, brittle rain lacing the windows.

Here we are, wondering how we are the ones

left. The ones still walking, still calling

so we can keep our narrowing web together,

posting on Facebook, making a path through

what exchanges the day requires, sighing

through each one because it's too easy

to forget times such tasks are beyond us,

when our bodies become canyons of pain

and its fatigue sets up camp and won't leave.

But here we are, still taking down the silent

decorations, setting Christmas trees

on fire to bless the coming of a year.

Second Line

38.


The simple answer is we haunt ourselves.

I'm listening to the stereo and slowly realize

everyone I can hear is dead and has been,

as are half the authors I'm reading

at any given time. I remember when

these were the names lighting the firmament.

The firmament is still there, but lit now by

new stars. Now the dead park in my yard

without asking, build fences along the property line,

tear them down and build them again, closer

this time. If I'm not careful, I'll talk about

nothing but the problems they cause until

it's easier not to talk. So I find

a record I've heard before and play it again.

39.


For years all I knew about Jesse James

was the song on one of my dad's records.

Later The New Riders of the Purple Sage

wrote a song called "Glendale Train" about

a robbery the James Gang pulled. By the time

I heard the song I'd read all I could find about

Jesse James and the rest of old west mythology.

By then my dad had new records, had found

the 70s singers like Croce and James Taylor

and had rediscovered Elvis. I thought of him

today when I tried to remember how

"Glendale Train" went, my dad's dusty records

my first lessons in law and history

and all that I would never learn about love.

Second Line

40.


Why do I keep ending up in graveyards,

waiting for some figure to announce itself

out of a fog bank that echoes the sky,

skittish with swift clouds that make targets

of the steadfast moon, the slow-to-burn stars?

After two weeks without a drink, I took

a shot of tequila without thinking,

then another till I was just high enough

to believe myself visionary. When

I walked home, I detoured through the graveyard

and lay for a while on the belly of a grave

and waited for something to happen besides

what did happen. I got up and finished

walking home, left the stones to their silence.

41.

The glass buildings glow all night, a shine

bright and artificial as the gloss

on a new dime, one more decoration

for a city intent on little more

than casting a greater light against

the thin shell of atmosphere, so we might be

even more visible from the air, a ring

shining in a display case. Almost thirty years

in this house while downtown quietly spread

from one tower to five or six with more

coming and more still resting on drawing tables,

sleeping on computers, waiting their turn

to rise out of dirt and noise so the city

I moved here to live in can keep moving.

Second Line

42.


A band's music can build a house you want

to live in, the slide of a trombone, cymbals

struck one time to conjure the nails, the scraps

of wood left when a project is done.

A house, like a song, never knows when

it is done until, one day, it just is.

But there is always some cleanup to do.

One horn plays the melody's sweet dancing

the way some homeowners paint shutters and doors

the blue of the birds they hope to lure

to their yard, decorations that come

and go at their whim. This is one reason

we go to music. It shelters us the way

we know home just by how it smells.

43.

Nobody alive ever heard Buddy Bolden

play. No record remains, no cylinder,

Only old men's talk and now not much of that.

Old men talk of ghosts as though they were still here

in their coats of flesh, still using air, leaving

tracks where they walk. Shadows invite us deeper

with each tale. Rust furs antique iron fences,

moss crawls up the shady side of stone.

Out-of-tune wind blows sharp though the fallen

and deep-piled leaves. If Buddy Bolden heard

such dwindling music, he would be tempted

to raise his horn, to play what he knows about

weather, time, the music there is no end of,

one more reason to call this place Storyville.

Second Line

44.


In college I had friends who could write papers

for class in a single night. It never worked

for me. Then, as now, I didn't know my thoughts

until I wrote them and picked my way through

the briared paths my brain pursues. I needed

time to sort through whatever topic

the professor rolled their eyes and agreed to.

So when I was up late writing, it was

nothing geared to help me in the marketplace,

as a student once asked me about Hamlet.

In a room as empty as a skull,

I scribbled while money went on being made

elsewhere. If it was too late or I was too drunk,

it would be a while before I knew what I'd done.

45.


It's dangerous out there for drunks and addicts.

Cops, higher prices, lower quality, all

the places you can't go anymore. When

I stopped drinking, going out began to require

some planning if I was going to stay

There had to be coffee, ginger ale. I learned

to turn my head to avoid whiskey breath

and struggled to hear the band above the drunks

singing different songs, all off-key. Home was safer.

My version of the world has gentled a bit.

Now no one drinks like they used to, even

when we make a toast and raise water, the odd whiskey,

glasses of diet soda to the ones not here.

Each year fewer of us can drink that toast.

46.


Time to let the band play, ain't it, Sir Clown?

When I sang "The Shakespeherian Rag" in class

some students laughed, others looked worried.

This is from a time without cell phones. This was

when we were still bringing in the sheaves,

blowing horns to the holy oracle,

breaking into churches to steal wine.

This was when blood was important. When

the music you listened to told the rest of us

who you were. This was before "The Waste Land,"

when words still slept in books. We thought we knew

what was coming, but we refused to look.

We chose a song and danced in the ashes,

danced till we no longer could.

47.

Some revelers paint their faces until

they are skulls. Thus disguised, they don scarves, hats

made to look like crowns, gaudy robes, bring drinks

down to the street where the bands play and those

who feel a certain way can join the parade.

Buddha reminds us to be patient, to live

inside each moment. Motion is the best way

I know to live inside time fully.

And wasn't that always the purpose of

the parties, the drugs and songs, the affairs

no longer talked about, even the workouts

and meditation, all of it to hold time

from moving so quickly and just for once

silence the rattling of our bones growing old?

Second Line

48.


To a building empty as a dead lung

came the farmers, their leaves already mortgaged.

It didn't take long working there to judge

the quality of the tobacco, which would

get a good price at auction, which had cooked

too long in the tin buildings used then to cure

the green leaves to a brown that fetched

money at auction. When the sale was done,

when the drinks were being poured, we took the floor,

hoisting the bales onto wheeled jacks, pushing them

to doors where trucks waited to take them

to Durham or Richmond or wherever

cigarettes were manufactured to sell,

and farmers lit cigarettes, each exhaling his small death.

49.

The drum is every child's first instrument.

Hand pound tabletops, spoons slap against bowls,

one body's effort to simulate

the motions of the heart. Bones can rattle

syncopation as well as any wooden sticks.

I've seen an old man take a pair of curved rib bones

and set them clattering in whatever

out-of-space time signature you can conjure,

holdover from the days when the animal's

every part was used. And the drum remains,

silent hammers of the arteries working

to push blood to the body's every outpost

and feet still tap to the shuffle and juke

of the song this world wants to be.

Second Line

50.


We were dancing somewhere and went outside

to smoke a joint. Forty-five years later,

someone calls to tell me you have died.

And I'm a bit less tethered than I was

to the universe. Even if we didn't

see each other or even speak often,

your presence gave the world some balance.

You read my first poor stories, talked with me

about books we both read—John Irving

was big that year—and showed me poems better

than anything I could aspire to.

When your husband died, when you moved down here

to your childhood land, I thought we would

talk more, but life has never been a poem.

51.

The job of the living is not to stand

or sit still. It is to get up, ready

to make that second line walk and not think

about the day they'll be walking for you.

Everywhere, loss and reminder of loss.

But you have to be alive to feel that loss.

Someone right now is chasing a melody

she has never heard before. Right now, someone

might be writing the book that will make us

put away our accounts and ledgers and take

our place in the assembly—did I mention

you're walking too?—as it moves forward

singing the name of the lost. I'm in back

seeking a pattern where others have walked.

Begun 2-21-2024


Finished 2-26-2024

## About the Author

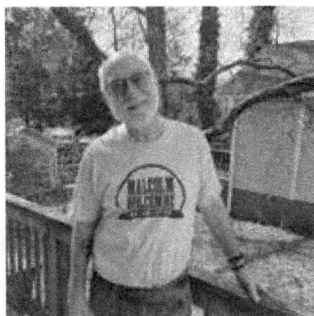

Al Maginnes was born in Massachusetts and grew up in several states. He has degrees from East Carolina University and the University of Arkansas. He is the author of fourteen collections of poems, most recently *Fellow Survivors: New and Selected Poems* (Redhawk Publications, 2023), and his writing appears widely. After nearly forty years of teaching, he has retired and now lives in Raleigh, North Carolina, where he tries new things and ponders what comes next.

www.ingramcontent.com/pod-product-compliance
Lightning Source LLC
Chambersburg PA
CBHW022041090426
42741CB00007B/1154